Visions

Visions Inspired through Spiritual Intelligence

Orville Douglas Denison

Archway Publishing books may be ordered through booksellers or by contacting:

Archway Publishing
1663 Liberty Drive
Bloomington, IN 47403
www.archwaypublishing.com
1 (888) 242-5904

ISBN: 978-1-4808-7969-0 (sc)
ISBN: 978-1-4808-7970-6 (hc)
ISBN: 978-1-4808-7971-3 (e)

Library of Congress Control Number: 2019908510

Print information available on the last page.

Archway Publishing rev. date: 07/05/2019

Preface

I offer my thanks and gratitude to my spiritual guide sources for my life on earth with great appreciation of all the magnificent people, especially my wife, Gloria Denison, and my children and grandkids. Cameron Schuyler, my grandson, is the artist who illustrated the cover of this book.

My life has been a sequence of visionary experiences. In the past, I have hesitated to tell people about them, having experienced reactions of disbelief, shock, and withdrawal when I have. I have grown to appreciate the blessings I have received and no longer care what people think of my story because it is true and beyond what many people think is possible.

I believe that many people are walking around with spectacular stories of miracles in their lives. But they do not have the desire to share because of the reactions they may receive. Spiritual intelligence is available to everyone, but some people do not visit that level of connection. Therefore, they do not believe that anyone can access it.

During a meditation session at the Global Truth Center in North Hollywood, the practitioner Lori Donato read the following statement from a *Science of Mind* publication.

> I am a spiritually intelligent being making divinely inspired choices.
>
> I am blessed with intelligence greater than my mental IQ-my spiritual intelligence. This deeper knowing guides me through any situation in life as I continue my life's journey, growing in wisdom and understanding. My spiritual intelligence reveals itself as intuition. If I am challenged by a circumstance, I say "Thank you, God" because I know I have been given an opportunity to evolve, spiritually.

Saved from Certain Death

The year was 1958. I was twenty years old. My first working experience out of high school was at All Season Awning Company in Los Angeles, where I met Ray Osowa, a fellow worker. Ray was an avid hiker who invited me to join him on a hike to Mount Wilson Observatory and see the ruins of a historic inclined railroad along the way. I invited my friend Larry Parret to join us.

We met at the corner of Lake Avenue and Calaveras Street in Altadena, which is the north end of Los Angeles, at the base of the mountains. Our plan was to hike up to the Mount Wilson Observatory and back in a single day.

Here's a little history. At one time, there was a magnificent inclined railroad. A cable system pulled cars up the incline to a transition point, where passengers transferred to another car and rode up a gentler slope to hotel accommodations. By the time of our trip, a fire had destroyed all the structures, leaving only their ruins. After reaching the hotel at the top of the incline and continuing to Mount Wilson Observatory, we returned down the same path.

At one time, a bridge structure had crossed a canyon, but it no longer existed. There was a vertical drop-off of about twenty feet to the trail below. We decided to drop our backpacks to the trail below and then traverse around until we could find a suitable incline to maneuver down to the trail. We would then walk back on the trail to pick up our backpacks and continue down to our car. About one hundred feet along, we saw a V-shaped gravel chute that looked like it would be easy for us to just sit in and push off from so that gravity could take us to the trail below. The gravel chute was covered with small rocks. We reasoned that it would be safe, even fun, to sit down and let the small rocks act like ball bearings.

Ray went down, and then Larry went down. It was my turn. I sat down, pushed off, and began accelerating, rolling along on the small rocks. As I slid down, my boot hit a protruding rock, which perhaps had been covered by the small rocks before but were exposed after my friends went down the chute. I was in a sitting position, and the inertia of my upper body went over center. So, I tucked my head under to protect my face. I tumbled right across the trail and somehow flipped over, landing facedown, with my chest in the middle of a small spanish bayonet plant. My legs dangled down in space. The spanish bayonet was the only thing not falling into the canyon below. I was fortunate to have landed on it. Otherwise, I would have fallen to my death.

The leaf edges were as sharp as a razor and cut my neck. Each leaf tip was like a needle and punctured my chest, arms, and neck. I lay there momentarily, with my upper body in the plant and my legs dangling into the void below. I was numb and in pain. I reached up, trying to grasp anything to pull myself up. Each time I attempted this, dirt and rocks fell into the canyon. At the same time, I tried to get a foothold, but there was nothing but a void below. It seemed like death was imminent.

I prayed to Jesus Christ with all my heart to save me. Then I felt at peace. I relaxed, looked up to my left, and saw Jesus (see book cover) in a light form. His image was about ten feet tall. He had a very serious, concerned look in His eyes. I was shocked that Jesus was there instantly. No words were spoken. He appeared and knew what had just happened. His image was illuminated against the evening sky and was much larger than life size, suspended in space.

I looked away, and then I felt a lifting force under my feet. I glanced down and saw a His large hand under my feet. I felt it lifting me. A moment later, I realized that I had been lifted up and onto the incline about halfway up from the cliff edge and trail. I looked up, but Jesus's image was no longer visible. Larry was staring down at me, motionless, not saying a word. Ray was standing on the trail above.

I yelled to Larry, "Throw me a rope!"

He said, "Oh yeah." He threw me a rope, which I grabbed, and he pulled me up the incline.

The three of us walked away without any discussion. I looked back and saw my red hat still on top of the spanish bayonet. I left it behind. We never spoke of this miracle.

Personal Comment

I surmise from this experience that in the spiritual world all things are known, especially when death is imminent. It does not take any time at all for the spiritual world to respond.

Here are some of my questions as a result of the supernatural experience:

- How did Jesus know that I would be in that precarious situation at that exact moment?
- How did Jesus in spiritual form have a solid hand that physically lifted me to the slope above the cliff?
- I prayed to Jesus and Jesus appeared and rescued me in the same moment.
- It is all beyond my understanding. From this experience, I have concluded that in the spiritual world there is no limit in time or distance. Response was instantaneous!

My Heart Stopped and Was Restarted

In midafternoon one day in 1982, when I was forty-four years old, I was lying on my left side in bed at home, about to take a nap, when I felt pressure building in my chest. My heart began to pulsate or flutter erratically. Then it stopped beating. I did not pray, yet the instant my heart stopped, two men and a woman appeared in the room in solid form, not light form. The men, dressed in suits, stood beside the bed, facing me. A woman, whose face was down at bed level, close to my face, intensely looked into my eyes—or my brain. I was alert and could see these people clearly. The woman's face moved closer and closer to my face. I was not afraid; there was a sense of peacefulness. As the woman's face came closer still, her face seemed to merge or disappear into my head. I felt an internal mild buzz or electrical sensation in my head. Then my heart began beating again. As my heart revived, all three people from the other dimension disappeared.

Personal Comment

- How did the woman and two men know that my heart would stop in that moment?
- Is the spiritual world monitoring me/us at all times?
- Is there some special reason I was revived?
- I wondered, *Should I accomplish something special?*
- I wondered why there were three of them.
- Was the woman the instructor and the men watching students? Or the reverse?

This book is not intended to be an instruction manual on how to access visions. Rather, it is about the visions that I have experienced in my life. I have illustrated many visions and collected published materials that match the illustrations as a source of validation.

Who Am I?

I was born in Durango, Colorado, on November 4, 1938. My mother, Ruth Denison, gave birth to my brother when she was sixteen years old and me when she was eighteen years of age. Grandma and Grandpa Jones migrated to Durango, Colorado, from Liberal, Missouri. They were farmers. Grandpa moved into town and started a business called Jones Wonderland. His business dealt with used merchandise.

Since Mother worked and went to school to further secretarial skills, she was rarely with us. There was no father presence. Grandma and Grandpa Jones provided us with a family atmosphere until I was four years old.

Mother was diligent in honing her skills to become a top-notch secretary. She had ambition and found employment in Lawrence, Kansas, where she had a brief marriage. The marriage ended within a year, after which we moved to Wichita, Kansas. Initially, I was terrified to move to Wichita, a big city that seemed intimidating. I quickly found that the city offered many opportunities.

I obtained a newspaper route, which I ran two times a day. It provided me with some income for model airplanes and violin lessons. Later, I took lessons on the string bass, or the stand-up bass. The junior high school orchestra accepted me as a violinist. I practiced diligently. Eventually, I played a solo at a music event.

The newspaper-route income also made it possible for me to afford a bicycle and later, a Cushman motor scooter in addition to music lessons. I also began making model airplanes and riding the bus to the weekly model airplane club, called the Wichihawks.

I entered Roosevelt Junior High School in the ninth grade. When I joined this upscale orchestra, I dropped violin and focused on string bass. After a short time, I challenged and obtained first-chair bass. In the summer following ninth grade, there was an open audition for students. An orchestra was being assembled to perform for the Music Educators' Convention in Chicago, Illinois. My junior high school director was one of the judges and asked for me to audition, so I did. I was assigned to second-chair bass. Our orchestra occupied two train cars. As an extra benefit, we toured Chicago in a tour bus. Being part of this orchestra and the association with other diligent students were great boosts to my feeling of being whole. The grand orchestra played before a large audience. The orchestra sounded very professional. My career in music continued through the years. Later, my music interests focused on jazz, big bands, and stage shows.

Early on, model airplanes were important to me. The challenge started with creating scale model aircraft for a competition in a hobby shop. Then I built free-flight kit planes but was disappointed in their performance.

I made modifications to some of the kit planes, which resulted in much higher performance. I joined the Wichihawks Model Airplane Club and became friends with other competitive kids, Boeing test pilots, Piper and Cessna design engineers, and other kids with a love for competition and airplanes.

Model Airplanes

My second set of challenges was focused on model airplanes because the construction, aerodynamics, and competition provided engagement that I did not receive at home. This provided a whole new connection with very accomplished people in engineering, pilots, and comradery with other kids.

At age thirteen, I built numerous model airplanes. The first one was a scale model of a jet fighter and then another. But I wanted to build something that would actually fly. So I built the kit planes in the picture. They did not fly as well as I wanted, so I purchased a gas-powered engine, an Olsen .23.

Then I built a free-flight plane on which to mount the new engine. It was remarkable how well it all came together. I bought a new smaller engine and put some parts together to make my own plane. The two planes enabled me to win two first-place trophies in the Wichita Eagle-Chrysler-Plymouth-sponsored international model airplane contest.

WIN DETROIT TRIP—Douglas Denison (left), 13, 2163 South Minnesota, and Leon Burlingame, 8, of 1821 South Battin, grinned happily when they were informed that they had won trips to Detroit to compete in the international flying model contest Aug. 20 to 25. The boys will go by car to the motor city and during their entire stay in Detroit will be the guests of the four local Plymouth dealers. They won their trips by having the highest number of points in the recent Plymouth-Eagle model airplane contest.— (Eagle Staff Photo.)

Detroit Trip Is Prize

Plymouth Dealers Announce Model Plane Winners Here

Winners of the trips to the Detroit international flying model eliminations in August were announced this week by the four local Plymouth dealers.

Traveling to the big Detroit meet after winning top places in the Plymouth-Eagle meet recently will be Leon Burlingame, 8-year-old modeler who captured first place in his age group for stunt flying at the local meet.

Douglas Denison, 13, 2163 South Minnesota, will accompany Leon to Detroit with all expenses paid by the four local Plymouth dealers. Douglas won first place for his age group in the free flight competitions which were held at the Mooney airport during the all-day contest recently.

Third winner of a trip to Detroit will be Sam Snyder, a Wichita modeler who took first in A-B speed tests and C-D speed competitions held on the huge parking apron at the Wichita air force base.

Point System Used

Judges at the recent contest picked the winners by points won in the various contests the modelers entered. The three boys now have a chance to compete with other top model flyers from the United States and Canada at the big Detroit meet.

Accompanied by representatives from the four local Plymouth dealers: Belford Motors, Inc., 550 West Douglas; Evans Motor Co., 235 South Topeka; Spencer's Auto Service Co., 1210 East Douglas, and R. D. McKay Motor Co., Inc., 1325 East Douglas. The winners will drive to Detroit sometime in mid-August just a few days prior to the meet.

Tour Planned

While there, the Wichita modelers will have a chance to see all phases of automobile production and will be guests at the airfield on the outskirts of Detroit where the contest is scheduled to be held.

Cash prizes and trophies are to be awarded to the winners in this Sixth International Plymouth Motor corporation flying model meet next month.

The Wichita winners of the Plymouth-Eagle flying meet will take the planes to Detroit that won them the free trip. However, they may build new ships to enter in other contests if they prefer.

Model Airplane Contest Winners Off for Detroit

The Wichita model airplane enthusiasts left early Sunday for the sixth international model plane contest in Detroit, sponsored by the Plymouth motor corporation.

They are the local winners of the Plymouth-Eagle model plane contest held at the Wichita air force base during June.

Receiving an all-expense trip to Detroit are Leon Burlingame, 8, of 1821 South Battin; Orville Denison, 13, of 2163 South Minnesota, and Sam Snyder, 20.

Accompanying the model flyers is Don McKay. The trip is being made by car, with side trips of historical and scenic interest.

The Detroit corporation has a well-rounded schedule for local sight-seeing and entertainment in and around Detroit, including a tour through the Plymouth factory

We traveled to Detroit, Michigan, in a new Plymouth station wagon driven by the local Plymouth dealer. Transportation and food were provided. We stayed in the Conrad Hilton Hotel. I felt elevated having won the trip and notoriety.

After moving to Wichita, Kansas, I was in the classroom with some excellent, encouraging teachers. Many thanks to them all.

Something triggered my visions at age thirteen. This was the first time I was in tune with the infinite and opened my mind to receiving infinite intelligence, although at the time I could not label it. Before going to sleep, in a relaxed state, I wondered what automobiles, aircraft, and various other objects would look like in ten or twenty years. I received light-form images in my head, and I found that I could control how I saw them. I mean, I could mentally suggest that the object rotate or I could look inside, and the vision would respond. I used this ability to envision new forms of aircraft design. I followed my visions and designed and built my own airplane concepts, which were very good flyers, and I achieved success in competition.

Table of Contents

A New World Order, and What Can I Do for You? 1

Helping One Another 8

Visions: I Saw My Deceased Father-in-Law 10

Visions: A Lost Puppy Projected a Vision of Her Owner's Face to Me 12

Visions of Aircraft 14

Lives That I Have Saved 16

Concepts Published 19

Brain Wave Transmission 22

Soap Bar Concept: Soap with an Identification Logo That Lasts the Life of the Bar 24

Vision: Cylinder-Shaped Hydrofoil, Santa Maria, California, 1962–63 25

Vision: Supercavitating Torpedo, 1963 27

Vision: Lifting-Body or Blended-Body Aircraft 29

A Variety of Automobile Visions 30

Autos without Wheels 31

Vision: Disabled Transport Vehicle 34

Vision: Auto with Rear-Facing Seat, 1963 36

Vision: Centrifugal Force to Linear Force, 1962–63 39

Stacked Building 41

High-Rise Concrete Construction Process 46

Self-Hypnosis Astral Travel in the Future Vision: Mining on Another Planet or Asteroid 47

Vision: Space Station 49

Past Lives 55

Pranks a Lot 59

A New World Order, and What Can I Do for You?

On June 19, 2014, I was driving home from Cortez, Colorado, to Monrovia, California, after visiting with my brother. After driving for many hours, I became very tired, so I stopped at a motel in Barstow, California, to spend the night. After I relaxed on the bed, visions of the future began.

The words "A New World Order" resounded in my mind, followed by, "What can I do for you?" Mental scenes followed. In this set of visions, God reprogrammed all humanity with a new mind-set where they no longer thought of self-first. A streaming vision of the reprogramming of humanity followed, with many scenes of the new mind-set. I could not determine whether this transformation was instantaneous or occurred over time. It seemed to be instantaneous, but in the spiritual world, there is no such thing as time.

How the Vision Was Received

Presently, we are programmed to be competitive and to accumulate more power, more money, more land, better cars, more jewelry, more property, more servants, and more control over others. More of everything. People will lie, cheat, steal, and even kill to obtain more money, thinking that more money brings more respect and happiness.

Some people use any means possible to achieve all these things without regard for the damage it does to themselves, other people, and the economy. Scenes with dialogue began to flow into my mind about the forthcoming changes. I thought that I should write down everything, but there was no paper in the desk. So I crossed the highway to a Vons market to purchase a pad of paper to make notes about the event.

I returned to the motel room and lay on the bed and relaxed. The vision continued. As the thoughts and words entered my consciousness, I began writing as fast as possible. Visions flowed into my head with scenes from many parts of the world.

It started with a stream of views of the direction the world was heading. Threats of war and nuclear attacks, which made it seem like the end of humankind and possibly of all living organisms, were possible.

"How can I help you?" became a dominate mind-set. I wondered, *How will that change the world?* Then the answer to the question followed. When we put others first, all human-to-human interactions will be altered.

Human Minds Have Been Reprogrammed Before

1. The Bible teaches that in the beginning, Adam and Eve had the ability to converse with animals. Later, after reprogramming, they could not.
2. I wondered whether this reprogramming event would be like the biblical description of the Tower of Babel, where humans once had a common language but could no longer speak the same language or understand one another.

   Wikipedia quotes the following biblical account: "Genesis 11:1 claims that prior to the event, humanity spoke a single language. In the confusion of tongues, this language was split into seventy or seventy-two dialects, depending on tradition."

People Will Compete Only with Themselves

The focus on sports will not be against another person. Rather, one competes against his or her own record. This concept will not be well received by almost everyone who enjoys participating in or watching competitive sports. Performing anything better each time is rewarding in itself, not at the expense of another person.

In the new world, there will no longer be a need to amass money or property, or to control other people. That all goes away when our mind-sets are to serve everyone with equal importance to our own needs. Our new mind-sets will be to find something good in others and complement them. We will ask them, "Do you need help?"

Help could be in crossing the street, lifting something into the car, offering your umbrella, helping to catch a loose dog, or anything that develops in your path. Happiness follows once you have assisted another person. Helping becomes the food of happiness.

Government Control of Funds

Military funds will be diverted to other purposes because maintaining a military force will not be required with the new mind-set. In my vision, leaders of every country realized that a majority of funds are used for military purposes and always have been. When political minds are redirected with the "How can I help you?" mind-set, money previously spent on the military will be used to

- pay off all mortgages (there will be no homeless people);
- eliminate hunger;
- provide everyone with medical care; and
- provide mental health care to everyone, including people with drug addiction and criminals in prison.

Other priorities for military funds include the following:

- desalinization of seawater so that everyone has pure drinking water and clean water for growing food (more on this later)
- medical-and-mental-health-targeted DNA directed toward correction of mental illness and physical illness
- education, language skills
- entertainment
- music and fun
- free prescription drugs

The Vision Continued

I saw corporate meetings and military strategy meetings interrupted by the reprogramming of their minds. In meetings, discussions about war strategies changed for everyone. They all became baffled, wondering how current programs would help anything or anyone. They realized that funds must be reallocated with the top priorities being health, housing, and happiness.

Anywhere in the world, groups of leaders gather around boardroom tables and joke about using resources to destroy people and property. That discussion suddenly changes to asking former enemies if they will join them in a feast and see how they can help each other rebuild bombed cities and help victims recover. Conversation moves to how to provide a quick setup or a renovated home for everyone.

Uniforms Will Be Eliminated

Titles and uniforms make a distinction between people. All uniforms will be abolished. Identification badges will have just the person's name and contact information.

All Borders Will Be Eliminated

Throughout the world, there will be no city, state, or country borders. Homes will be located by coordinates. Instead of countries or borders, the geographical GPS numbers will be used to identify locations. Homes will be referenced by longitudinal and latitude coordinates. GPS systems will divide the locations down to several digits for longitudinal and latitude coordinates.

This process eliminates positive or negative associations based on country or city. When a person moves to another location, their ID spot changes with them as they go.

No one would be lost by moving to a new number. We will all get along better because we won't judge others as being from another country.

Moving will not require selling or buying a property. Just investigate the list of available properties and sign up for them between certain dates. And then move. The listing for the prior property will move to the available list. When settling down, the listed date can be indefinite.

Native Americans knew that you can't own land. The settlers talked to them about owning property, but Native Americans knew better. Land is only here for you to use for a limited time because life on earth is limited. We should have a use permit.

A World Information Center Available to Everyone on Earth

A world central computer system will collect data on assets and on where they can be applied to resolve human need. Materials and products will be inventoried into a worldwide sourcing database. Those in need will only have to ask. No money will be exchanged.

Data will be organized so that needs are quickly filled. Aircraft, ships, and ground transport trucks will be made ready to move supplies to areas that need the supplies.

Organizations and/or individuals will post notices of the required service, or individuals or groups can post what services they can provide. Databases will be scanned, and appropriate persons will be connected to the solicitors. Skilled and unskilled persons will read the postings and respond.

Training will be an ongoing process. Skilled persons will train the unskilled in every capacity.

Desalinization of Seawater

On a Mediterranean beach south of Tel Aviv, Israel, a vast industrial facility hums around the clock. It is the world's largest modern seawater desalinization plant. It was built by the Israeli government.

Desalination Enterprises, or IDE Technologies, uses a conventional desalinization technology called reverse osmosis (RO). Thanks to a series of engineering and materials advances, it produces clean water from the sea cheaply and on a scale never achieved before, demonstrating that seawater desalinization can be cost effective and provide a substantial portion of a nation's water supply. Under the new mind-set, seawater will be desalinated for drinking and to provide water for growing crops. Desert areas will become plant- and food-producing areas as well developed for homes. The new supply of water does not require large reservoirs, only water storage tanks.

The supply of water can be pumped from the sea to the water storage tanks using solar, wind, or wave power, depending on the area.

Competitive Contact Sports Will Be Abolished

Injuries such as brain trauma, broken bones, organ trauma, and even death can be attributed to impact from boxing, football, soccer, and other contact sports. Lives can be completely altered when two bodies collide with force. The "How can I help you?" mind-set precludes any harm that one person will intentionally do to another. People will only compete with their records, not against another person.

Other Changes

Television broadcasts will only provide positive information, such as instructional and inspirational events and stories, where people can meet, how they can acquire new skills, and learn about health, music, planet beauty, and cleanup. Lists of projects and jobs will be posted. Stories about travel, sea life, and constructive and challenging events will replace murder and horror programs.

People with limited physical abilities will have responsibility for providing some services, such as watering and feeding plants and trees, which will be used to beautify the landscape. Having the responsibility and performing a task well brings happiness to each person. The job will be tailored to the capability and interest of the individual. As skills grow, the person will be offered new, more challenging tasks.

As mentioned earlier, focus on the military will change. Military ships will be repurposed. They will be redesigned to accommodate people for transportation, into hospital ships, cruise ships, floating hotels, housing, entertainment, and accommodations for those with handicaps.

Ships will contain education programs for all ages and college levels with firsthand experience for those seeking careers in diplomacy and other world culture careers.

Military helicopters will be converted into multipurpose units. Some will be used as firefighting units. Others will be used to transport people from land to aircraft carriers and other repurposed ships. Helicopters will rescue people from oil rig platforms when weather threatens.

Submarines will be used to study sea life, learn how sea creatures communicate with each other, find medical cures, and for rescue operations. Other submarines will be used as underwater cruise ships, with observation windows to see sea creatures and underwater terrain.

Aircraft carriers will be used to carry helicopters and firefighting aircraft for quick response to disaster situations. They may also be used for cruise ships. The deck would be fenced with tables on the surface and other entertainment venues.

The Food and Drug Administration (FDA) will be dismantled. The focus in medicine will change from treating to curing illnesses. The high price of medicine will be minimized to small profit margins.

Ammunition will be destroyed, so guns will be useless. Weapons will be melted down and the raw materials put into a resource stockpile to be used for applications worldwide.

Prisons will be transformed into productive environments, such as teaching or medical institutions. Inmates will apply and be evaluated for jobs. They will be released because of their new positive mind-sets and productive objectives. Theft and crime will be replaced by "How can I help you?"

Tests and grades will not be used in the education of inmates or in general education. People who desire to learn another language will carry a pocket translating device, so they can go to any country and immediately communicate with the people there.

Police stations will be shut down. No need for that service. Inmates will be directed to facilities where they can watch videos about the many trades and services they have the opportunity to learn and perform. Serving brings them happiness as it does to those they help. Their instructors find happiness in the progress of the inmates. No one will be working for another person. Rather, everyone works to do their parts to help the whole of humanity. No one is above or below another.

Persons who were previously unassociated with a job will go to a place where they can look at the needs within their communities and find a service they can provide after attending workshops. Entry-level jobs could elevate to more involved jobs as exposure to the conditions and education increases. Anyone can move to another part of the world to work with people who have a mission with which he or she identifies.

If a person has no experience, rather than taking a handout, the recipient of the food and shelter would provide a service to the provider, such as cleaning floors, taking out trash, cleaning windows, or growing plants and trees. A person could contribute by educating others with lesser skills.

No one will want to impose his or her ideology. All people will see the differences and admire the way those differences have evolved. Cultural specialties will be showcased so others can admire them and appreciate their development and history.

Gas stations will not require a payment system. Just push the button, and gas will flow. The only readout will be the on or off. The gallons of gas taken will appear on the pump display for inventory purposes.

Utility meters and parking meters will be removed. Water, gas, and electricity are all provided at no cost. Water will be resourced from the ocean and rivers via RO.

Helping One Another

An older man notices that an even older woman is struggling to move a small pallet of water from the stack to a shopping cart. The man picks up the pallet of water bottles and places it on the lower rack of the elderly woman's shopping cart. The woman says to him, "I love you," and the older man says, "I love you too."

A man sees a woman with three kids sitting on a bench. He wonders if they might need food or clothing. He had just come from the store and has some apples. So he offers the woman and kids an apple each. They are thankful. He directs them to the store where they get more when they are hungry. They are new to the area did not know about the store. They thank the man.

Local officials are changed and take responsibility to see that there are no cold, hungry families on the street. People previously unassociated with a job will go to a place where they can look at the area's needs and find something they think they can do for the community. Signs will be posted, directing people to community services and shelters.

Jobs will be posted on an international register. If a person is not associated with a job, rather than just a handout, he or she will offer to clean the floors, windows, and sidewalk in return for food. This gives the person a sense of pride and fulfillment. Nothing is given with an expectation of something in return. Return services are given because people want to help. A store owner might just look out and see a man cleaning his front window. The store owner and the man cleaning the window both feel the blessing, and both are happy for the experience.

Groceries will be scanned, not for money, but for inventory control purposes only. There is no identification necessary, and there is no money exchanged.

Let's say a doctor provides treatment for a musician. The musician might come and play music for the doctor and his guests. His guests might consist of clients and associates. The musician might then play for patients in the hospital to speed their recovery. Actors will come to hospitals and perform for the patients who appreciate the entertainment as they might fee; they've lost out on the pleasures because of confinement.

"How can I help you?" eliminates discrimination. And the Internal Revenue Service (the IRS) is eliminated as income accountability is not a factor.

Education will be free and desirable because it makes it possible to know how to help more and in new ways. There will be no charge for books or instruction. Lessons can be downloaded and completed anywhere.
A variety of subjects will be listed so a person could choose a field based on perceived talents and capabilities.

An invention center will open to accept new ideas that can benefit humanity and animals. It will include divisions that explore how to grow plants to supply food for people and animals that do not promote illness and disease.

In wars of the past, land mines were planted. Ever since, people have been killed or had limbs blown off because they were never been removed or detonated. Although the war in that area may be over, the land mines still exist and continue to kill and injure the residents of the area.

Engineers will develop a flying ground effects drone that will have powerful downforce of low frequency sound waves that replicate a vehicle traveling over the road. The vibrations would cause detonation of the land mine. The explosion would eliminate the drone, but it would eliminate injury to people. The machine will hover over ground or water. The round detonator drone will draw air in through an opening in the top. Fans will blow the air downward, creating a cushion of air on which the drone can travel over land and water without contact with the surface. Controllable air vents permit directional control, so the programmable unit can cover the entire roadway and areas of land beside the roadway. The detonations will enable safe travel in previous war zones.

Visions: I Saw My Deceased Father-in-Law

Many years ago, I was cast in a stage production of *Cinderella* in Pasadena, California. Scott Lawrence was the producer and director. After the play closed, there was a cast party at Scott's house.

Three of Scott's friends were seated on a sofa across the room from me. My wife, Gloria, and I were sitting in a row of chairs facing them. Gloria sat on my left and was chatting with someone in the chair to her left.

I was looking at the people sitting on the sofa. My wife's deceased father suddenly appeared in solid form, standing behind the sofa. He wore a three-piece suit. Lawrence Hansen had passed away years before.

He stood there, staring at Gloria. I turned to Gloria to see if she saw her father's image or presence. I looked back at him. His eyes were fixed on Gloria. I looked back and forth at him and at her. After about thirty seconds, he disappeared. On the way home, I told Gloria about seeing her father.

We wondered why Lawrence appeared. It occurred to us that he may have been trying to communicate with Gloria to contact her sister or half-brother. The next day was a Sunday. Gloria called her half-brother, Doug Hansen, in Fernly, Nevada. At the time of the call, Doug was performing some repairs on the roof of his double-wide manufactured home. He came down from the roof to talk with Gloria. They talked for a while, and everything seemed fine. Still concerned, she placed a call to her sister, who was also fine. We dismissed the vision.

On Monday, Doug Hansen was driving home from his work in Reno, Nevada, traveling east toward Fernly. One of Doug's coworkers was driving directly behind Doug's pickup. Suddenly, he saw Doug slump over toward the passenger seat and out of view from the rear window.

The truck went out of control and crossed the recessed dirt median between the freeway lanes. Then it went down the slope on other side and stopped in a ditch below. Doug's coworker called for an ambulance. A helicopter arrived and took him to a hospital in Reno. Unfortunately, Doug had a heart attack and transitioned.

It seemed obvious that my vision of Lawrence Hansen the Saturday before was for Gloria to make immediate contact with her brother, before it was too late. I surmise that spiritual people know when and where death will occur.

Visions: A Lost Puppy Projected a Vision of Her Owner's Face to Me

One day I went to work, and one of the employees had a small dog in a box. My coworker said she was hiding in the bushes outside the factory. The adjacent street was a very busy boulevard.

Several people in the office offered to adopt her. Two employees took her home for a day or two to see if she would be compatible with their families. Each time the puppy was returned to the factory for one reason or another.

I saw her and instantly felt a connection. I took her home for a compatibility trial. I put her in the box, placed the box on the passenger seat of my truck, and drove toward home. Occasionally, I glanced down and saw her looking up at me. I saw love and intelligence.

As I drove home, the little dog rested in the open box. I looked into her eyes, and her face was suddenly superimposed with the image of an African American woman's face. The woman's hair was in braids and pulled back around her head. After a second, the woman's face disappeared, and I saw only the dog's face.

Several days before, the employee who found the dog had placed a "Found Dog" advertisement in the *Pasadena Star News* in an attempt to find the dog's owner and return her.

The next business day, I opened the entrance door to the factory. Inside, I saw the woman in the lobby. Her face was exactly the same as the image that the little dog projected to me, except she did not have braids, and her hair was down. She was holding another dog that was the brother to the one I had taken home. The woman had seen the advertisement, and they were waiting for me to come to work. I was dumbfounded and heartbroken. I told her about the experience of the little girl dog projecting her face to me. She said, "It is understandable. We are a very spiritual family." I also mentioned that in the vision, her hair was in braids. She said, "When the dog went missing, my hair was in braids." I promised that I would go home after work, pick up the puppy, and bring it to her. She gave me the address. That evening, I delivered the little dog to the woman. Her young son was delighted to get the dog back. But I had already fallen in love with the puppy.

After thinking about how much I wanted her, I called the woman and offered to purchase the dog for a hundred dollars. She said, "It is my son's dog. It would be his decision." She also said her son was at a friend's house, so she gave me the phone number, and I called there. I offered the boy a hundred dollars for the little dog. He agreed and said he could get two dogs from the SPCA animal rescue with the money and have some left over.

The boy then asked if I would also take the brother because he did not want to separate the two dogs. My wife and I agreed and happily adopted both dogs. The best two dogs ever. We named them Muffy and Jeffie. We gave them love for their entire lives. Sadly, they have returned to their Creator. I give thanks daily for the pets we have loved in our lives.

Visions of Aircraft

During World War II, bombers like the B-17 and B-29 had four wing-mounted radial engines. In the early 1940s, my brother and I went to the movies often. Newsreels featured war zones around the world. I recall one in particular that showed a B-17 over Germany, which was attacked by German fighters. The film was shot from an adjacent American bomber. The German fighter shot one outboard engine on the bomber. As one engine stopped, the plane went into a spiraling nosedive. The thrust on one side was greater than the other, which contributed to the wingover and loss of control.

I meditated on that issue and had a vision. I saw jet engines attached to the rear of the fuselage on either side and a third jet engine inside the body on centerline.

I drew the vision and presented it to Colonel Tibbets, my mother's friend. He passed my illustration on to a Boeing engineer. The engineer visited me at our home and asked questions about the centerline jet engine and how the air inlet duct would serve the engine inside the tail of the aircraft. I told him it was an S-shaped duct. He acknowledged and took my additional drawing with him.

The result was many jet passenger planes evolved to mounting the jet engines to the fuselage, just as shown in my drawing. (FYI: Colonel Tibbets was the pilot of the *Enola Gay* B-29 that dropped the atomic bomb on Hiroshima and ended World War II.)

Lives That I Have Saved

Saving lives is being in the right place at the right time and taking action, while disregarding fear or possible harm to myself.

Number 1: Durango, Colorado (My Birthplace), 1949

My brother and I were on vacation, visiting our grandparents in Durango, Colorado. Frankie lived a half block away.

One day, I walked over to see whether Frankie was home. He was, so he and I decided to go for a walk and explore the outskirts of Durango. We came to a railroad bridge that crossed the Animas River.

We decided to walk across the railroad ties to reach the other side of the river. Why? It seemed like a challenge.

As I stepped from one railroad tie to another, I made the mistake of looking down through the space between the ties. When I saw the river moving swiftly below, I experienced vertigo, or dizziness, which sent a bolt of fear through me.

I focused on the ties and tried to ignore the movement of the water. Frankie was ahead of me, stepping right along, apparently not bothered by vertigo at all. We both made it safely to the riverbank on the other side.

Frankie walked ahead of me along a path that paralleled the river. He had taken only a few steps along the pathway when the embankment broke away, and he fell into the river. He was splashing and yelling for help! He was moving rapidly because of the strong current. Adrenaline shot through my body. I realized I had no rope or any way to reach him. I ran as fast as I could along the riverbank path until I passed Frankie. Then I saw a small tree, about an inch in diameter, growing on the bank! I pushed the tree over into the river and yelled to Frankie to grab the tree, which he did. I pulled Frankie out of the river using the tree like a stiff rope.

Frankie was soaking wet. I asked, "Well, what do you want to do for excitement now?" We laughed.

Number 2: Wichita, Kansas

In 1952, my friend Chloe Aikin, her younger brother, two friends of hers, and I went on a picnic alongside the Arkansas River in Wichita, Kansas.

Chloe's friends drove us to the river's edge in a Ford Woodie station wagon (the Woodie had wood trim on the body panels). The driver of the car and his girlfriend were Chloe's friends and were about seventeen years old. Chloe and I were about thirteen years old, and Chloe's brother was about nine years old.

There was a sandbar peninsula that projected into the river. I walked out on the center of the sandbar and could see the river on both sides.

Chloe's little brother ran out onto the sandbar while we were unpacking our picnic lunch. We heard him scream for help. Chloe and I turned and saw that he had fallen into the river from the tip of the sandbar.

The river was not swift like the Animas River in Durango, but nevertheless, as he moved only a few feet downriver, he was already ten feet out from the shoreline. Chloe was a good swimmer, but she panicked and froze as her brother floundered.

For a moment, I did not know if I should swim out to him or wait to see if Chloe was going to save her brother. Chloe looked petrified and made no motion that she was going in after her brother. In a couple of seconds, I took off my shoes and socks. I sprinted out to the tip of the sandbar and swam quickly to him. It took only a few strokes to catch up with him. I rolled him over on his back, so he was face up. Then I firmly pulled his head up under my left armpit. He was very cooperative and did not resist. I used my right arm and scissor kicked back to the bank. Although it was only about ten feet out, we were drifting downstream. Swimming was difficult because I was wearing a shirt and pants. It took all my energy to pull him to the shore. When we reached the bank, I was completely exhausted, unable to stand.

Chloe and her friends were standing on the river's edge, waiting for us to reach shore. They grabbed her brother and lifted him out of the water. Then they took him to the car. I was left at the water's edge, dripping wet and exhausted. After a while, when I could stand up, I picked up my shoes and slowly walked to the car. The picnic was cancelled, and we went home. A festive event it was not.

Number 3: Downtown Los Angeles, 1970

I was employed at Barker Brothers' Furniture store as an assistant buyer. Each morning I parked my car in a lot a few blocks from the store and walked to the office. As I was walking toward the store, I heard a fire truck with sirens screaming and the lights flashing just a half block away. Then I noticed an elderly woman began crossing the street in the crosswalk. She did not hear the fire truck. She was apparently deaf because she continued to shuffle into the crosswalk. Each step she took seemed calculated, as if it might be painful to walk.

My adrenaline pump was working fine because my heart raced as I ran out into the crosswalk. From behind her, I placed both arms around her waist and lifted her off the street, stepping backward as fast as possible. She screamed when I picked her up. Lifting her was not easy because she was much taller than I am. The fire truck never slowed down. It just missed us by just a couple of feet. The woman saw the fire truck as it screamed by us. Then she relaxed. Until that moment, she must have thought she was being mugged. I released my hold on her and put her back on her feet, near the curb.

The funny part of this is that an old man watching us from the sidewalk clapped his hands and yelled, "Way to go, sonny!" I laughed.

Number 4: Near San Diego, California

Gloria and I were visiting a friend near San Diego, California. Our friend's mother was in the kitchen, snacking on something when she started gagging. Then she stopped making any noise. She appeared to be ready to collapse to the floor. Our friend screamed, "Someone to do something!"

I raced over and positioned myself behind our friend's mother. I put my arms around her waist, clasped my hands together, and pulled upward into her abdominal area, attempting to perform the Heimlich maneuver. My first attempt failed, and she went limp. With all my strength, I again pulled upward into her abdominal area with my fists. She coughed up some food and started breathing normally to everyone's great relief.

Concepts Published

In January 1955, *Air Trails* magazine ran a design competition called "Young Men of Vision." I was awarded second place. They published my twin jet-twin tail interceptor. Many years later, fighter jets evolved to the identical concept from single jet-single rudder to the twin jet-twin rudder as I conceived and was published.

AMA National Record Set

I built a series of original hand-launched gliders in various configurations and shapes with less than astounding performances. Some of them had elliptical-shaped wings. Other configurations, called canards, had a stabilizer in front. And others had high- or low-aspect ratio wings.

One day I visited my friend Larry, who was an engineer and a member of the Wichihawks Model Airplane Club. He built a hand-launched glider with an elliptical-shaped wing and triangular airfoil. I watched him launch it. It did not perform as well as he expected, and I wondered how to improve on the triangular airfoil.

My vision was to change the shape of the wing from elliptical to a double sweep-back with a higher aspect ratio (longer and not as wide). Important: The wing high point radiused around the tip, which produced lower turbulence. We moved from Wichita, Kansas, to Long Beach, California, in 1954. I had just entered high school and located a local model airplane club. They informed me about an AMA-sanctioned contest at Los Alamitos Air Force Base. I arranged for a ride to the contest and entered.

My flight total was high enough to break the national record for all age groups. They requested that I draw a set of three views of the original glider, which were included in their annual publication.

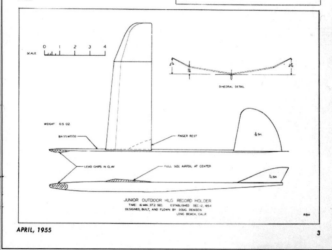

not exceed 7 pounds."

Speaking of boo-boo's, we've already found a big one in the new AMA rule book. It's on page 15, item 15 under section 14.15. The first line should read "Consecutive *Outside* Loops" instead of "Consecutive *Inside* Loops." Clip out the box below and paste it to page 27 of your rule book. As additional corrections or interpretations are made, it is suggested that you do likewise.

> Correction to page 15, item 15 under scection 14.15, *"Inside"* in first line should be *"Outside."*

FAI Sporting Codes are now available from AMA Headquarters. A complete set consists of Section 1 (general rules pertaining to *all* sporting aviation) and Section 4 (particular rules for model aircraft) Each section is priced at 50¢, so the charge is $1.00 for the complete unit.

If the following symbol appears now or beside your name and address this issue, this is notice that no more issues will be received by you on your present subscription.

4-55

Since no further notice will be given of your expiration, it is important that you look at this column regularly.

MODEL AVIATION is the monthly news bulletin of the Academy of Model Aeronautics and is "The Independent Voice of American Aeromodeling." Published by the AMA at 1025 Connecticut Avenue, N. W., Washington 6, D. C. Editor: Carl R. Wheeley. News and photos of club and contest activity always welcome for publication. Copyright 1955 by the Academy of Model Aeronautics. Permission is given for reprint or quote provided source is given. Subscription rate to non-members is $1.00 per year. For subscriptions outside the United States, add 50 cents for postage. Entered as second-class matter at the post office at Washington, D. C.

SCALE 0 1 2 3 4

DIHEDRAL DETAIL

WEIGHT 0.5 OZ

BASSWOOD

FINGER REST

LEAD CHIPS IN CLAY

FULL SIZE AIRFOIL AT CENTER

JUNIOR OUTDOOR HLG RECORD HOLDER
TIME IS MIN. 37.2 SEC. ESTABLISHED DEC. 12, 1954
DESIGNED, BUILT, AND FLOWN BY DOUG DENISON
LONG BEACH, CALIF.

I followed my vision of the design by building and flying that concept. The record exceeded all age groups.

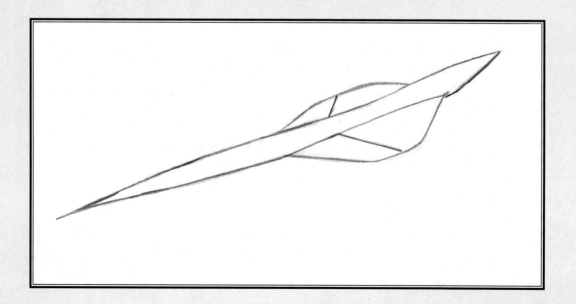

Brain Wave Transmission

In 1962, I saw a television program that showed how the eyes and ears transmit signals to the brain, which are then interpreted as images or sounds. Like many other visions from my life, I asked, *How will this evolve?* I saw a variety of developments, including how movies would involve all the sensations from the person being recorded and a second person would be able to see, hear, and feel the exact sensations. Many things could develop from this, such as an airline pilot's movements and sensations would be recorded into a black box. In the event of a tragedy, the exact feelings and sensations could be observed by anyone who could receive the impulses generated by the pilot.

Let's say person number 1 went bungee jumping with the recording gear on. Person number 2 could experience all the sensations of the first person. A disabled person could experience all the sensations of an athlete, including running, swimming, skiing, and even sex.

A trip to Mars could be transmitted to Earth, and the first and second persons would be able to see, hear, and feel all the same sensations.

Vision: Population Control: Sperm Control Valve

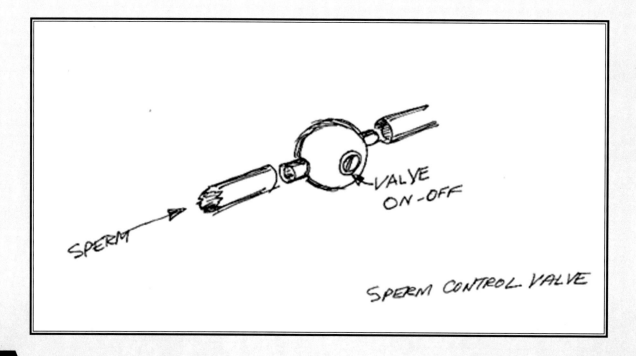

If all men had their sperm blocked by a controllable valve, there would be no unplanned children. Children would be born into homes when the couple was ready to provide mental and physical nourishment and guidance and to plan for their education.

Abortions would not be necessary if a sperm valve were implanted in the male prior to puberty. There is a critical point in the development of the male when a sperm control valve could be surgically implanted, which would block the flow of sperm.

The sperm control valve would be set to the off position on insertion in the vas, preventing sperm from flowing out of the penis. When parents are ready to raise a family, a simple procedure under local anesthetic in which a small incision is made and the valve opened would enable the flow of sperm. The valve can be turned off again when the desired family size is reached.

Soap Bar Concept: Soap with an Identification Logo That Lasts the Life of the Bar

One day I noticed that the brand name was recessed on the surface of a bar of soap. After a few uses, the recessed brand name washed away, leaving only the shape of the bar for identification.

The vision that followed was to make a mold so the logo, or brand name, was cast in one color the full thickness of the bar. The logo could contain another chemical and color. For example, it could be a different color with a fragrance or skin softener. As you use the soap, the logo never disappears.

Vision: Cylinder-Shaped Hydrofoil, Santa Maria, California, 1962–63

While employed at Boeing, Vandenberg AFB, near Santa Maria, California, I became aware of hydrofoil boats. The functionality was to attach wings with struts to the boat. At a certain speed, the wings produced enough lift to raise the boat out of the water, thus reducing friction and enabling higher speeds. The craft was intended to have military applications.

Unfortunately, while the craft is flying along, there comes a critical speed where the water separates from the wing. That event is called cavitation. It means that the wing or wings lose lift, and the boat hull suddenly falls back into the water at high speed. In some cases, the hull might tumble, depending on how the bow enters the water. Therefore, it is critical to maintain a speed below the cavitation point.

I meditated on the wing and cavitation. I wondered, *How could a wing or lifting surface pass through the water and not lose lift?* A vision formed in my head. It was a cylinder rather than a wing. I visualized water entering the front of the cylinder and going out the back. No matter what speed, the flow would be the same. The cylinder would be adjustable for attitude and direction. When the nose of the tube was at a positive angle, the water passed through the tube, and was deflected downward. This produces lift, the action and reaction principle. Lift is produced, same as the wing, yet the water cannot separate from the tube because it is passing through a contained cylinder.

I built and tested the theory on a model boat that traveled over seventy-five miles per hour. On my test boat, there was no evidence of loss of lift. I filmed the event, and you could clearly see the space between the boat and the water at all times. The test boat flew silky smooth. You get the benefit but not the disaster.

I submitted a report of the test to the company I worked for. The concept was rejected. I took the film and the report to the base commander, the highest-ranking official on the base. He did not understand the rejection notice either, so he called officials on the patent staff, higher up in the company. The base commander reported to me that they did not want to pursue my concept and lose their existing research funding on their inferior wing (even though their wing was limited in speed by the cavitation or separation principle). The patent staff was only interested in the continuing flow of money from the government per an existing research contract. The cylinder concept died.

More variations of the tube hydrofoil came to my consciousness. The tubes could have an expansion chamber at the rear, where a mixture of chemicals could cause a ramjet-like thrust when they were ignited, expanding the gases as well as the water. The result would be considerable forward thrust and lift.

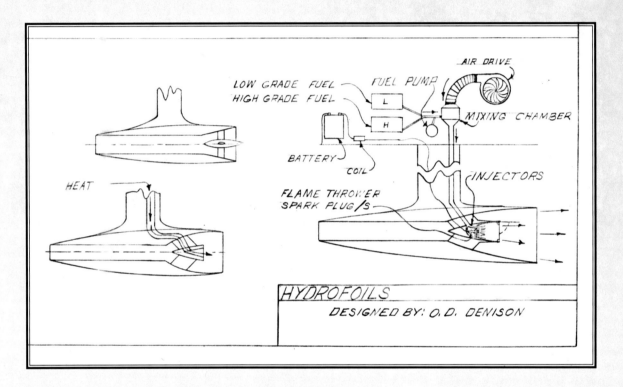

HYDROFOILS

DESIGNED BY: O. D. DENISON

Vision: Supercavitating Torpedo, 1963

Could cavitation be used to one's advantage? A series of visions came to me. First was a torpedo with a tube extension from the body and a small cone on the tip. The conical tip forces the water to expand causing a large void through which the body of the torpedo can pass through the water with considerably reduced friction. The second version included a jet of compressed gas shot forward to blow open the cavity through which the torpedo could pass with reduced friction.

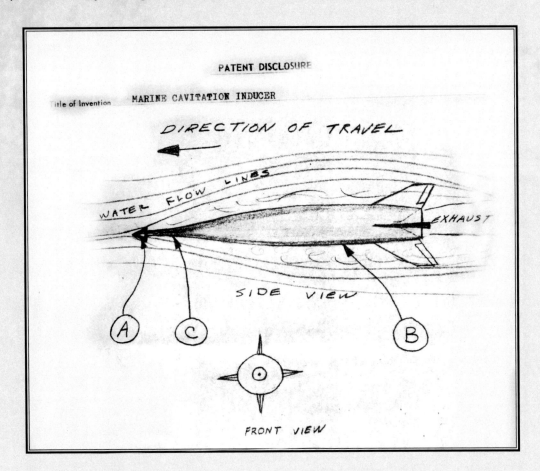

Popular Science magazine published a very comprehensive article with multiple pictures that clearly show the supercavitating concept. My concept submitted to Boeing in 1963 is identical to the concept illustrated in the June 2004 issue (pp. 66–67) issue, which claims speeds of more than two hundred miles per hour. The article can be found at https://www.popsci.com/scitech/article/2004-06/supercavitating-torpedo.

According to Popular Science Magazine, Russia developed the Shkval VA111 torpedo in the late 1960s. Their torpedo became operational in 1978. Since 1978, Russia has since sold the concept to Iran and other countries including Russia, South Korea, China, the United States, and Germany have been working on the concept. Apparently, there is no defense for this new super-fast torpedo. In the same article, they claim that China is working on a superfast supercavitating submarine that could go from Shanghai to San Francisco in a hundred minutes.

By searching on the internet for Supercavitating Torpedo you can see a YouTube video of a supercavitating torpedo hitting a warship and breaking it in two pieces.

Vision: Lifting-Body or Blended-Body Aircraft

Aircraft normally have a round or pencil-shaped body that does not produce lift. When the body is airfoil shaped, it produces lift while increasing efficiency and speed and improving fuel economy. I envisioned and illustrated the following aircraft, which incorporates this principle. The concept is being reviewed and tested in the recent past.

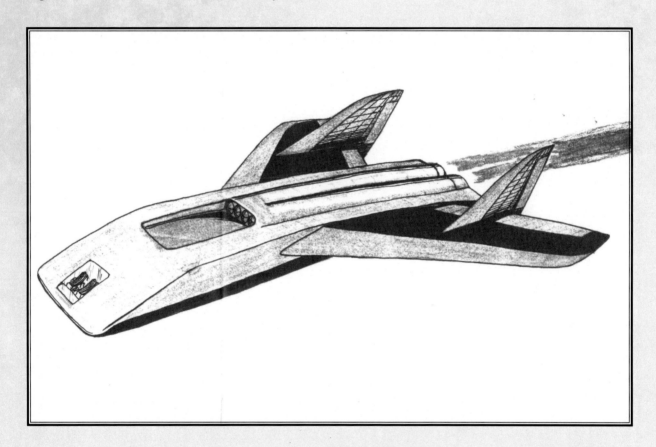

A Variety of Automobile Visions

One evening when I was thirteen, I lay on the bed and wondered, *What will cars look like in ten years?* Suddenly, the vision of the car illustrated below appeared in my mind as a light-form image. I saw it from the front view. Then I considered, *What does it look like from the rear?* The vision rotated at my suggestion! I zoomed in to see the details of the interior.

I illustrated the front and rear views. I kept the drawings. After about ten years, I was amazed to see the Italian-built car shown below in an auto magazine. It even had the same slots in the fender fins! I was amazed that an image would appear from a mental question!

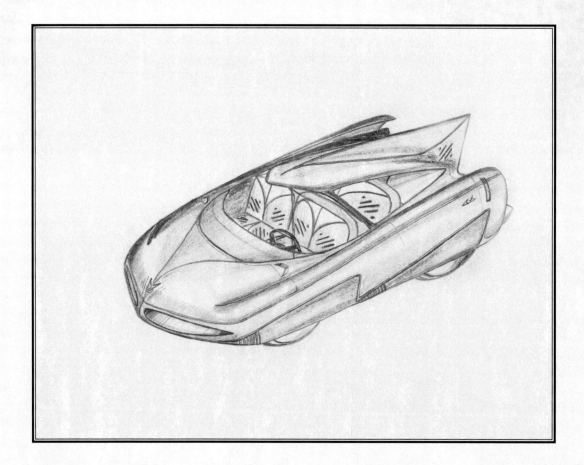

Autos without Wheels

In about 1951, a series of visions came to me of autos without wheels. I had no clue about what suspended them above the ground, yet they seemed as real as any other car concept. I drew what I saw in my meditations.

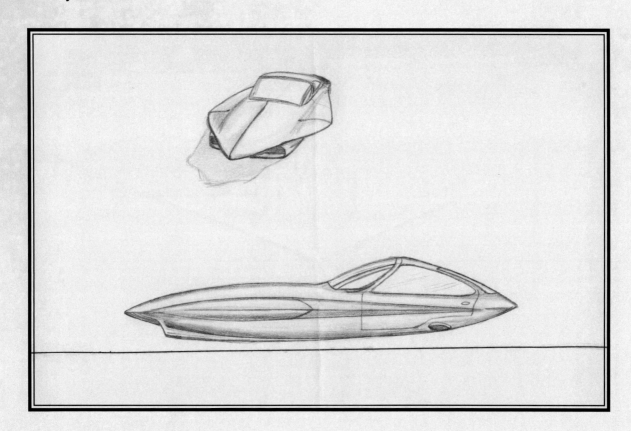

Vision: Auto with a Fuel Cell

The term "fuel cell" did not mean anything to me in 1953. I wrote the term on the drawing. The car below had one wheel in front and two in the rear. Notice the absence of a steering wheel. The headlights are strips along the front of the vehicle. There were only round headlights at the time this was illustrated.

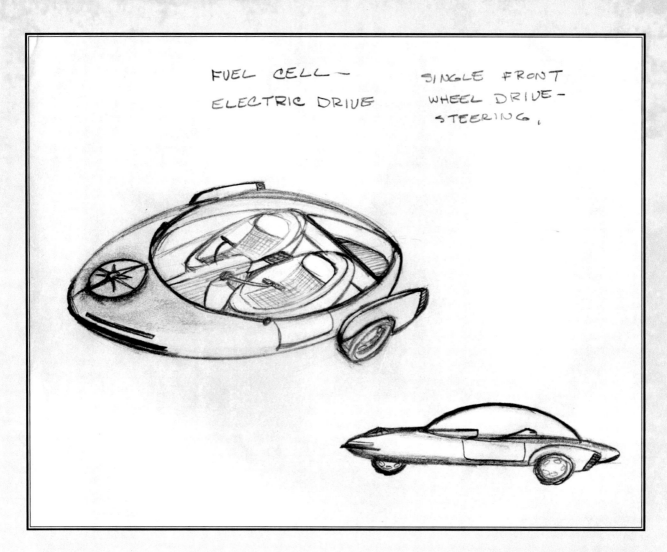

FUEL CELL —
ELECTRIC DRIVE

SINGLE FRONT
WHEEL DRIVE —
STEERING.

Downforce Wing

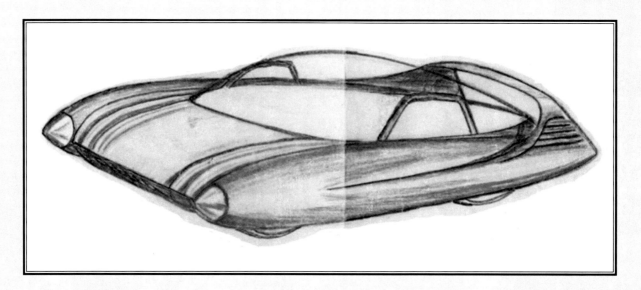

Years later, Dodge introduced a car with a downforce wing. Many racing teams added it to their cars to provide additional adhesion in turns and braking at high speeds.

Raised Headlight and Taillight Pods

When I drew this in 1966, I had no idea what kind of headlights would fit into the raised pods. Today, LED lights would fit nicely in the raised headlight and taillight mounts.

Vision: Disabled Transport Vehicle

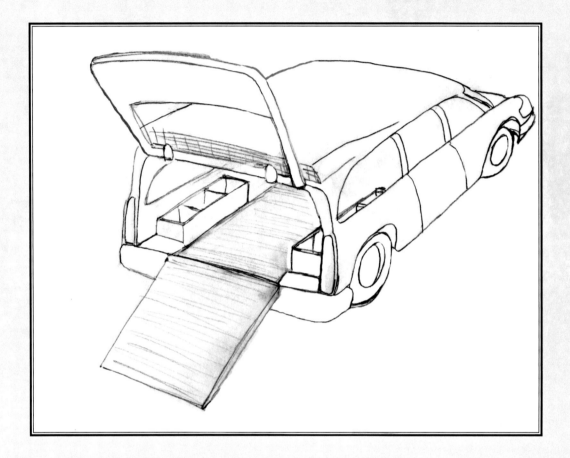

One day I watched a wheelchair-bound person navigate the angular ramps at intersections. As he went along and went down the angular ramp from sidewalk to street, he nearly tipped over. I wondered why a vehicle had not been developed that would permit safer travel and weather protection yet enable the person to remain in the small three- or four-wheeled vehicle that could travel inside stores.

I envisioned a combination of the small electric vehicle being able to enter an over-the-road vehicle. The combination would be safer and provide a freedom to travel anywhere. It would require a rear hatch that would open. Then a ramp would extend and drop to ground level. The small vehicle would drive up the ramp and forward to the steering wheel. At this location, there would be a powered rotating platform on which the small electric vehicle would rest. Clamps would come in from both sides to engage the small electric vehicle, keeping it locked in place during travel. It would disengage on command.

After the over-the-road vehicle arrived at a destination, such as a grocery store, and parked, the ramp would extend and drop from the rear hatch. The platform on which the small electric vehicle sat rotates so the small vehicle can come down the ramp and go anywhere. This exit system would work as well when arriving at home and entering a garage.

Inside the over-the-road vehicle, there would be bins along both sides, where sacks of groceries could rest during transit. When not needed, the bins could rotate up and expose a seat, where passengers could ride.

This vehicle concept would enable wheelchair-dependent persons to travel anywhere, park anywhere, be liberated, and live independently.

Step 1. Remotely activate the rear hatch to open and the ramp to extend and drop down to the pavement.

Step 2. Drive the wheelchair up the ramp to the center-front of the vehicle.

Step 3. Clamps with gripper pads come in from each side to lock the wheelchair so it cannot be moved.

Step 4. The motorized ramp is retracted, and the rear hatch closed. The operator is in complete control and can drive anywhere.

Step 5. Once the vehicle has reached its destination, the round base rotates so the wheelchair faces the rear for disembarking.

Step 6. The rear hatch is opened, and the ramp is extruded and dropped to the ground.

Vision: Auto with Rear-Facing Seat, 1963

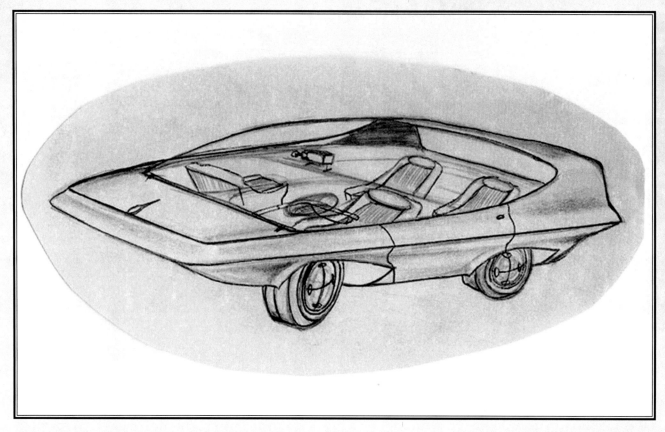

Notice that the front seat swivels to face the rear. This would be a safety feature that would protect a baby. When a child is not present, the seat could swivel around to be front facing. There is no steering wheel. Rather, a handlebar is used.

The August 2017 issue of *Motor Trend* magazine featured the Jeep Yuntu concept vehicle with a seat that faces the rear on page 20. The caption below the pictures states that this version is not intended for the US market.

Truck/Recreational vehicle

The concept for this vehicle is as an executive field operations luxury mobile office with chilled water supply, tools, and roof hauling of plywood and lumber. Rear fender storage is provided for refrigerated water, with a second chamber for tools.

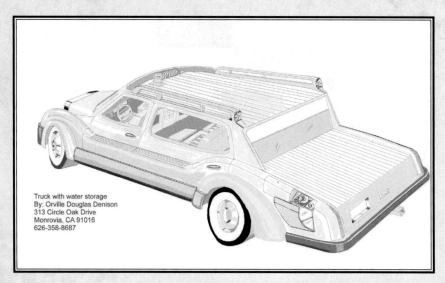

Truck with water storage
By: Orville Douglas Denison
313 Circle Oak Drive
Monrovia, CA 91016
626-358-8687

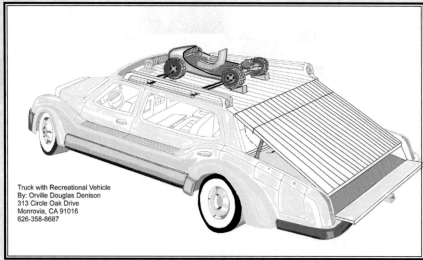

Truck with Recreational Vehicle
By: Orville Douglas Denison
313 Circle Oak Drive
Monrovia, CA 91016
626-358-8687

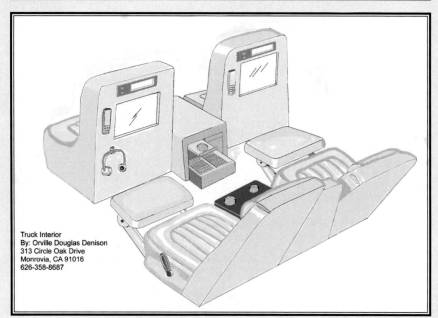

Truck Interior
By: Orville Douglas Denison
313 Circle Oak Drive
Monrovia, CA 91016
626-358-8687

The rear trunk area is a powered inclined lift. The top-mounted power winch clamps onto a sheet of plywood and pulls it up to the roof. This could be applied to a truck.

Vision: Fishing Boat and Floating Trailer

This trailer is designed to float, enabling it to be backed to the water's edge. The construction is of fiberglass outer and inner surfaces with a urethane foam core. There is a winch with internal battery for power. The boat can be released while in the water.

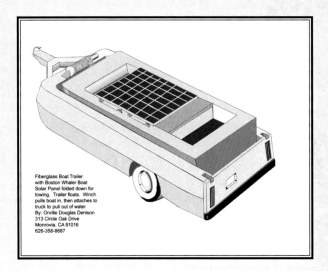

Fiberglass Boat Trailer
with Boston Whaler Boat
Solar Panel folded down for
towing. Trailer floats. Winch
pulls boat in, then attaches to
truck to pull out of water
By: Orville Douglas Denison
313 Circle Oak Drive
Monrovia, CA 91016
626-358-8687

Solar Roof, Electric Outboard Motor

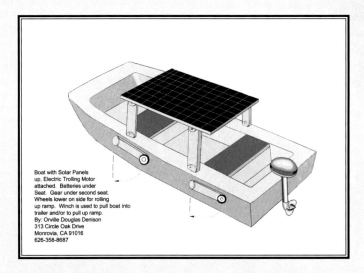

Boat with Solar Panels
up, Electric Trolling Motor
attached. Batteries under
Seat. Gear under second seat.
Wheels lower on side for rolling
up ramp. Winch is used to pull boat into
trailer and/or to pull up ramp.
By: Orville Douglas Denison
313 Circle Oak Drive
Monrovia, CA 91016
626-358-8687

The vision of this boat came after seeing an outboard motorboat on a lake, emitting pollution in the form of exhaust. Some lakes prohibit boats because the pollution kills fish.

This boat is solar-electric with a battery under one of the seats. There is a chiller for drinks, food, and catch under the rear seat. The trolling motor is nonpolluting electric driven.

Vision: Centrifugal Force to Linear Force, 1962–63

MANUAL POWERED
SPACE CYCLE
IN LOW
RESISTANCE
GRAVITY FIELD.
DOUG DENISON

Rotating mass creates centrifugal force which could be controllable for direction and liftVisions

Prefabricated Buildings

These buildings would be constructed of molded, double-wall fiberglass with a foam core. Electrical wiring would be built in with attachment points at the joints.

Separate living quarters with protected tunnel to central living area.

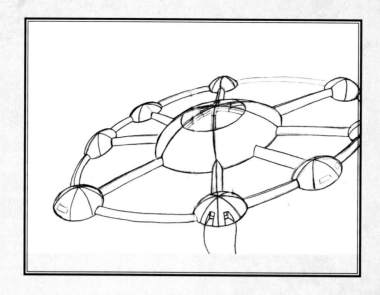

These are factory-manufactured structures with dual wall fiberglass construction and built-in wiring and plumbing. Or it could be manufactured using 3-D printing of concrete. It can be delivered to a site and connected to utilities in a short period of time.

Buildings with Underwater Restaurants

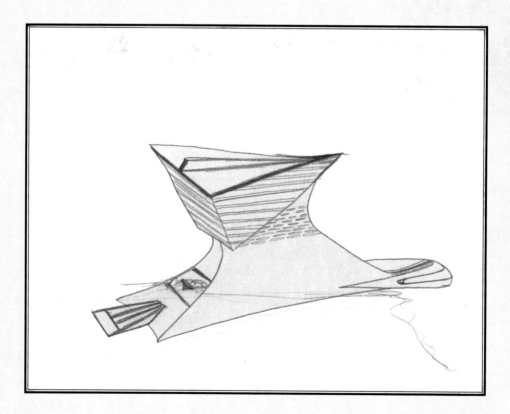

Stacked Building

A streaming vision with motion and sound was revealed to me in three parts. First, the tower of disk living quarters, ellipse in cross-section. Views in any direction. Nothing exposed to neighbors above or below. Cross-helical beam construction with welding at intersections made a rigid tower. An elevator moved up and down in the center of the vertical tube. Each living unit had a key that let them stop on the resident's floor. All others must get access permission from the floor owner.

When the vision started, I was inside a building, looking outward. The first thing I saw was a compound curved glass that was power opened, having a top and bottom rail system. The curved panels slide along the rails, exposing an unobstructed view of the landscape.

As the vision continued, I looked down and saw an igloo-shaped restaurant. It was a dome with an entryway. A spur from a railroad track came right up to the entry. The spur branched off a continuous track that followed the landscape and disappeared in both directions. As a train came by, one car disengaged from the main train and traveled down the spur, stopping at the foot of a restaurant next door.

The dedicated railroad spur stopped at their entrance.

Later, another train approached from the opposite direction. As it passed, the car that dropped off earlier accelerated and synchronized speed with the passing train so that it seamlessly attached to the train and left the area unified.

Weather Control, Third Part of the Vision Sequence

This streaming vision appeared much like a telescope housing. The curved slot exposed a cannon-like component that raised up and swiveled 360 degrees around the base.

In the same series of visions, I saw a formation of clouds in the distant sky. A slotted cover slid open, and a cannon appeared. It raised and swiveled around the base to aim at the sky above.

A whirring sound emanated, which increased in pitch and volume. Suddenly, bursts of electrical discharge popped and crackled in the sky above. The distant clouds were attracted to the location of the discharges. Rain began to fall on the land below. After a time, the ground absorbed a certain amount of water. Then the housing swiveled so that the gun was pointed to a location in the distance. Then another electrical discharge shot into the distant sky. The clouds were attracted to that location. When they arrived at the location of the discharge, it began raining.

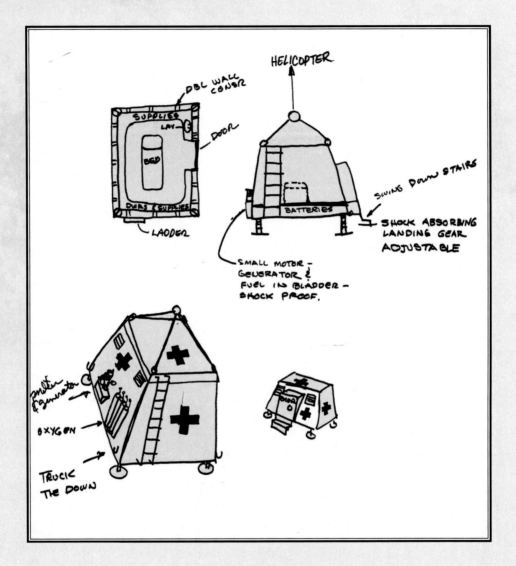

I also envisioned a completely self-contained portable emergency operating room. Potential uses would be in war zones or disaster areas. The double wall, urethane foam core, fiberglass walls provide structure and insulation. Resins could be made with fire-resistant properties. Cables molded into the structure provide a cradle to the hook on top, which a helicopter could use to fly the unit in and out. It could also be placed on a flatbed truck.

All molded inside and outside fiberglass with foam core.

Fiberglass Furniture

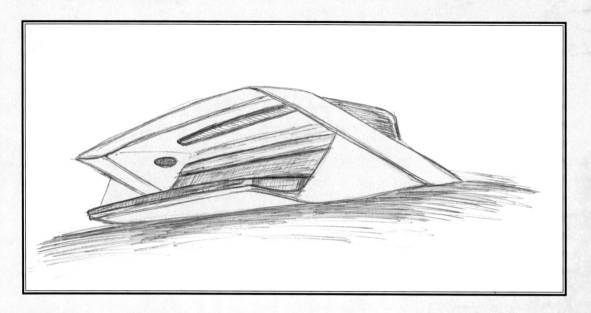

Stereo Speaker Systems

Stereo speaker systems with vertically mounted speakers. Drawings and production of obelisk wood and textured fiberglass speaker system. Finished speaker made with high-density plywood construction with textured surface of polyester resin and cabosil. Rigid construction and very little cabinet deflection means more projection of sound without distortion.

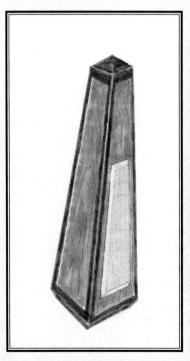

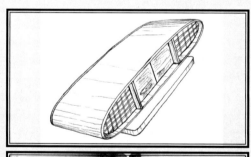

Boats

Visions of boats with corrugated fiberglass structural panels.

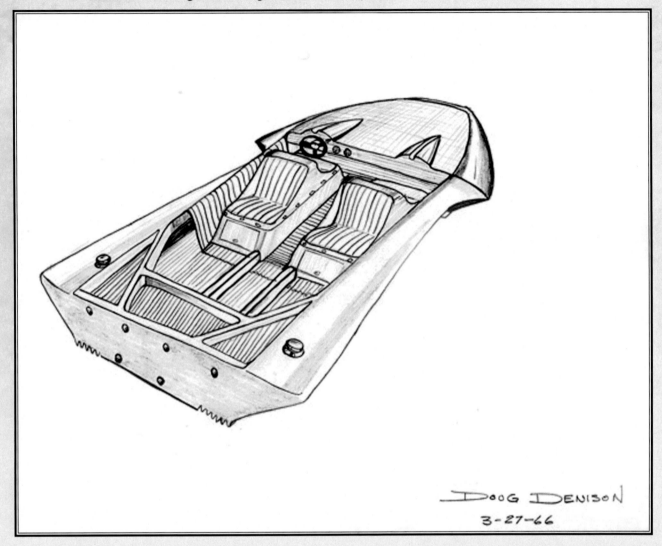

DOOG DENISON
3-27-66

High-Rise Concrete Construction Process

Fiberglass dome forms were used to create a waffle-pattern structure by pouring concrete over a group of forms. After the concrete has cured, the forms are removed from the concrete from below. As the forms were released from the concrete, they were permitted to fall to the ground, thus damaging the flange. This resulted in considerable cost increase to replace damaged forms. I had a vision of a new way to process the forming. Rather than removing one form at a time and letting it fall, I saw multiple forms on a pallet and removing them all at once. I illustrated the concept and submitted it for consideration. The president of the company liked my idea and told me so. He patented the concept and sold the company based on the value of gang stripping. Another vision validated.

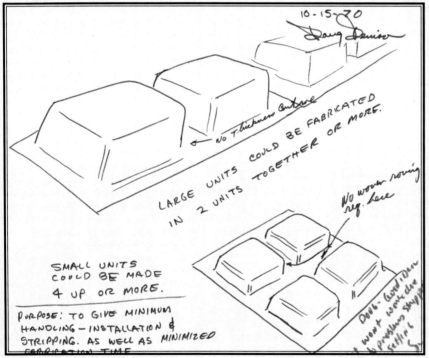

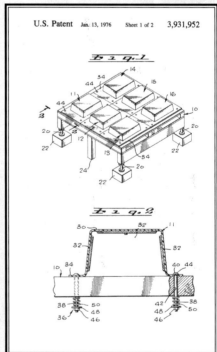

Self-Hypnosis Astral Travel in the Future Vision: Mining on Another Planet or Asteroid

This vision was like watching a video with sound. My vantage point was from above and some distance away. There were giant crystals of various colors sticking out. Below, I saw a mountain range that curved around. There was a flat desertlike area in the arch of the mountain range. Two tanklike machines came from behind a mountain range on the right. Both machines were remote controlled. The first machine came across a flatland and moved into a cove of rock with an abundance of crystals. It had a pick on the end of an arm that was retracted.

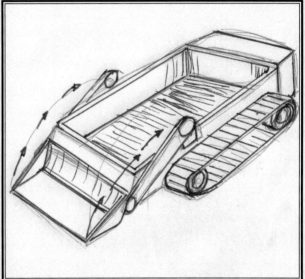

The first machine moved up to a contact point of the crystal rock. The vehicle stopped. A whirring sound increased in pitch, much like a motor or a gyro spinning up to speed. Suddenly, the pick slammed down into the crystal. Pieces of crystal broke away and fell to the ground. The pick vehicle moved out of the way, and a scoop vehicle moved into place. A tambour-type cover retracted on the top of the vehicle, and a scoop was exposed. The vehicle moved around, scooping up the chunks of crystal and loading them into the bed. The process repeated. When the bed was full, both vehicles returned via the same route from which they came.

Construction of the Pyramids

I gave myself a suggestion to go back to a time when the pyramids were under construction. A small group of men were instructing another group of men on the operation of a machine. The machine consisted of a large crystal and an adjustable sound-frequency generator. The sound focused through the crystal.

The first mode was set to slice or cut through stone. As the beam passed through the stone, it sliced a perfect line, regardless of the size of the stone.

The second setting diffused the focus, so it did not cut the stone. Rather, it excited all the molecules, making the stone vibrate so that the molecules were in suspension, not connected. The stone became weightless, much like water being vaporized into a cloud that then floats in the air. When it condenses, it becomes water again with considerable weight.

In the dispersed state, the crystal was moved, and the stone was lifted in the direction the crystal was pointed. The stone passed effortlessly through the air, just like a vaporized cloud. The crystal was lowered, and the stone was lowered into place on the pyramid. Then, as the sound generator was turned off, the molecules in the stone stopped moving and solidified, becoming the multi-ton object that we see now.

If the stone needed trimming, the focus of the sound generator was tuned to slice or cut, and the stone was easily trimmed. I wondered where the instructors came from and where they went after they provided training. What happened to the machines? Was this technology destroyed?

Vision: Space Station

In 1962, I had a very clear vision of a space station that rotated at a speed where the people walked on the outer wall with their heads toward the center. As the circular portion rotated, it created centrifugal force to the outer wall, so people could walk continuously in the loop. In the center was a round focal area that focused the sun's rays on to a plate. The plate was in a chamber and could be maneuvered so that it concentrated the sun's rays on the plate. That generated heat that could be used for the space crew, and the outer chamber could be used to generate thrust. It had a conical adjustable stopper that could plug the hole or move away from the exhaust hole. To add thrust, water was injected into the heat chamber, which would expand. As the pressure built, the stopper retracted and propelled the vehicle. The original drawing has been lost.

Vision: Slide to Safety

After the 9/11 Twin Towers disaster, I was very disturbed that more than three thousand people died in the event. Many could not descend the vast number of stairs to the exit. My vision was the Slide to Safety, patent 7,191,869: March 20, 2007. It consists of an inflatable slide, one for each staircase level inside the building. This concept provides quick escape with very little effort, regardless of the number of floors in a building.

Vision: Transportable Rescue Conveyor

I called it TRC-1, for transportable rescue conveyor. It was conceived to eliminate fire fighter effort to climb up a <u>one-hundred-foot ladder</u> with 70 pounds of suit and gear and to rescue people without the effort of carrying them down to the ground level.

Able persons would just step on a rung and hold onto the rung above, and then ride up or down. Disabled or injured persons would be placed into a rescue bag with oxygen. The bag attaches to the rungs above and below. The person can ride down without assistance from a firefighter. Therefore, burns or injuries are not compromised by handling. The oxygen provides life support in smoky or toxic gas environments.

On arriving at the bottom of the conveyor, at the level of the rescue vehicle, the person in the rescue bag is released from the bag or if necessary, transported in an ambulance while still in the rescue bag.

I illustrated the TRC-1 concept and patented it. The concept was published in a few magazines.

Existing aerial firetruck manufacturers did not want this invention to be successful. If the concept were successful, it would jeopardize their production, their inventory, and their investment and could potentially put them out of business.

Should be: The following two pictures are of TRC-1, the first patented version

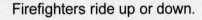

Firefighters ride up or down.

Firefighters ride up without effort. Rescue bag with oxygen.

Version 2: Transportable Rescue Conveyor
Patent 8,074,767

The rescue bag enables unassisted transport of injured persons. They are placed in a protective bag, with oxygen. The bag is attached to the rungs of the conveyor system. They are transported down at two hundred feet per minute.

3-D printed model, fully functional, shown in Baltimore, Maryland.

Version 3 TRC-3 Rescue Cart Patent 8,322,489

Third vision for external rescue from buildings, rivers, and the sea when mounted aboard a rescue ship.
By using two powered cable systems controlled with a closed-loop servo motor on each, the cables can control the position and speed of the moving cart to enable very fast deployment (approximately two hundred feet per minute) to positive or negative angles of the extension system.

The cart can be used for powering firefighters quickly to any level within reach. The return trip is equally fast, so rescue of firefighters and injured are very fast. Other uses of the cart can be, but are not limited to fitting it with a remotely controlled water cannon, a remotely controlled machine gun for operations on ground or at sea to detour pirate ships.

Victims can ride down even though they may be disabled, injured, or unconscious. No rescue bag is required.

This concept would cost far less than previous concepts because of the elimination of the take-up system and its lighter weight. Less ladder weight means less outrigger support. The simplicity and low weight makes it feasible to have two systems operating side by side. One could be fitted with a water cannon and the other used to rescue people.

Riders are completely protected from mechanical harm, gasses, heat, and flame. Benefits include lighter weight, more reliability, lower cost, and retrofit ability to existing fire truck chassis.

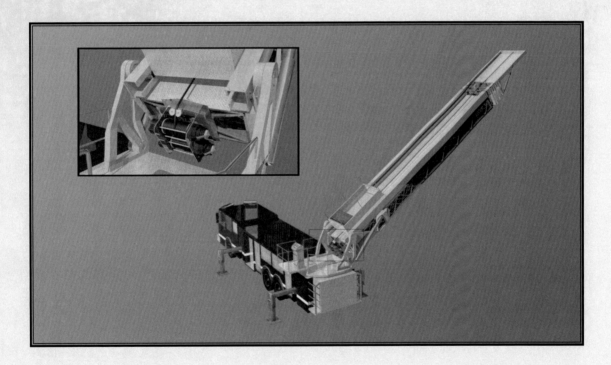

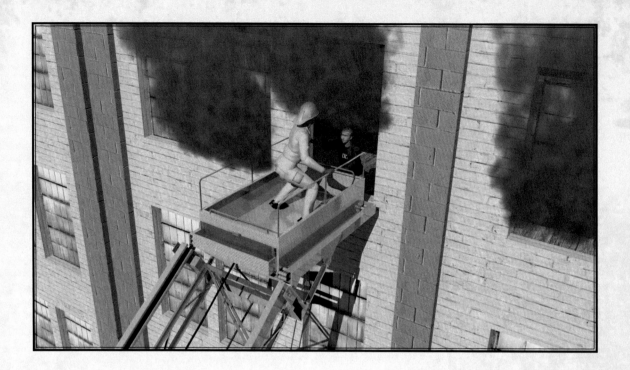

The inset picture shows how simple the system is for controlling the speed and position of the cart. Just two motors with closed-loop servo motors, and the cart is pulled by cables. There are no belts. No take-up system is required, so the cost and weight are reduced, and the possibility for retrofitting existing fire trucks is increased.

Rescue cart tips to horizontal for loading and unloading.

Past Lives

My wife and I attended a psychic convention early in our marriage. In one tented area was a group being instructed on using self-hypnosis. I sat down and responded to the time regression suggestion instruction. As the suggestion was given, I visited multiple past lives.

1. I visualized being inside a castle with exterior walls that appeared to be about three feet in thickness. There was a fireplace and a canopy bed. I was taken by the incredible detail in the fabric of a chair. I zoomed in on the fabric. I had a feeling of being somewhat restricted to that room. I felt like I was not among friends and had a cold and lonely feeling about being there. Then the director of the event instructed us to regress to the life before that.

2. I saw my arms, which were black. I was a baby and felt that I died shortly after the birth. On to the life before that one.

3. Then, going back to a life before that, I was an opera singer. I was on center stage, singing to an enormous audience. The auditorium had four elaborate balconies that curved in a huge radius. As I sang, a man in the front row stood, pointed a pistol at me, and fired. The bullet hit me in forehead. I heard the sound of the impact inside my head.

4. Before that life, I was in a longboat. As I was leaving, I saw a woman on the shore waving to me. We were setting sail. After we were at sea, I climbed the mast to look out. I returned to the deck, and a group of men was standing there in a confrontational style. One man stepped forward and engaged me in a protest. About fifteen men stood behind him and looked on anxiously. The leader challenged me. The group of men on deck were all about five feet six inches in height; I stood about six feet and eight inches. I was very strong and had a muscular build. The group leader faced me and angrily engaged me. I felt fear! I reacted by throwing a single right cross and hit him across the jaw. He dropped like a wet rag. Then I picked him up over my head and threw him into the sea. He sunk into the water. I turned to the group and asked who was next. They all turned and went back to work with their oars. They called me Eric.

5. One of the time regressions was to a place where tigers roam. I was walking along with one on my right side. My hand was on his back, at his front shoulders. As we walked along, I felt his shoulder bones move under my hand. We were companions. I don't recall the color of my arms, but the feeling of the shoulder movement is the important memory. I have always loved tigers and see that they can become companions to humankind.

Personal Thought Regarding the Past Lives

I recently felt that some of the actions I took to the detriment of other people have carried through from one life to the next. Realizing this, I have prayed for forgiveness for any harm done to others in past lives as well as in this one. In Jesus's name, I prayed. I immediately felt a calming and sense of purpose. Until now, I could not understand why I would be gifted with all these visions yet not be able to develop them. I now know that good will come from them and I will be happy that I have lived long enough and having been spared death twice to bring this book to you. I suggest that you consider your past lives and offer your thanks for understanding them, and if any harm was done to others, you pray for forgiveness and repent from doing any harm to anyone in Jesus's name. I know that you will be divinely guided, and good things will come to you through kind people. Love out and love back. Action and reaction.

Time Travel: Before the Beginning

Through self-hypnosis I gave myself the suggestion to see the earth at the time dinosaurs roamed the planet. The vision streamed with many views. The atmosphere was very, very dense with moisture. So much so, that water was dripping constantly all over the planet.

The earth was in a circular orbit, closer to the sun than it is now. A day of full rotation took only about four hours, which means that the surface speed was considerably faster, and the centrifugal or outward force neutralized much of the gravitational force compared to our present rotation. That is significant because animals of all sizes moved much more freely than they do now. We have seen the large dinosaurs lumbering around like a slow elephant. That was not so. Offset by centrifugal force, their body weight was far less.

Since the earth's orbit was closer to the sun, surface and atmospheric temperatures were higher. The atmosphere was like a very thick, dense fog. Imagine the water that is now the oceans being mostly in the atmosphere. There were some lakes but no oceans as we know them now. The short day and closer exposure to the sun kept the moisture mostly airborne, not cooling down much in the short night.

Vegetation grew in enormous volume as is obvious by the coal, oil, and natural gas deposits. Dinosaurs did not have to go far to find an abundance of plant growth for food. Birds of the day flew constantly, gliding on the constantly rising thermals of hot air and moisture. The wings and bodies of birds had hair like feathers that enabled moisture to leach off from their wings. Birds had only to open their mouths to take in food and water as they flew.

Vision: Self-Hypnosis Space Travel to Saturn

In 1967, after reading a book on practical self-hypnosis, I performed a countdown from ten to one with the suggestion that I would be at the rings of Saturn.

As I counted down, I felt as if I was sucked through a thin tube to a location in the pathway of Saturn's rings. I arrived in a superraised state of consciousness. My vision was limitless. Everything was brilliantly illuminated. I controlled what I saw with mental suggestions.

I arrived seeing chunks of material flying by, and they were enormous. From pictures I had seen of the rings, they seemed to be made up of small particles. My point of vision as I stopped at the location was directly in the path of the rings, and a mountain-size pieces were coming directly at me at a very high rate of speed. They passed through me, but there was a sensation as they did. It was frightening! I willed to rise above the rings, and was now looking down at all of them. It was a sight I will never forget.

My spiritual attention turned to the planet. It appeared as a ball of light with a gaseous layer. It did not seem solid. I was intrigued and formed a mental suggestion to go through the gaseous layer. As I passed through, it appeared as a thick, dense layer of some crystal particulate material.

On the inside of the sparkling outer layer, I felt as if I were inside a huge ball, looking back at a shell from the inside. There was a void between the outer gaseous layer and the core.

The core was an unbelievably large mass of very high-density crystal. For some reason, I came to the conclusion that it was crystal in nature by chunks of material slamming together with great force. The magnetic force was so great that it attracted my visual or spiritual self into it without my suggestion. I panicked. I was desperate to return to my body and get out of the force field of the core.

Suddenly, I felt the reverse of the travel to the planet; I was being sucked back into my body through the small tube. It took a nanosecond to travel from the planet to my body. And I slammed into my body with so much force, my body actually bounced up from the bed. Perhaps from muscular reaction or from the force of the spirit coming back home to the body. Who knows?

I had the most terrible headache ever, and it lasted for about a week. The experience was terrifying yet brilliantly illuminating.

Pranks a Lot

Family History and Pranks from My Youth

My First Airplane, 1944

My first airplane had everything: wings, propeller, tail, elevator, and first-class passenger accommodations. My brother and I knew it would fly, so we decided to test fly it from the second-floor balcony of our aunt Hattie's back porch. We spun the propeller on the front of the wood box and then pushed it off the balcony. It was transformed into a pile of wood scrap. Later, I learned about aerodynamics!

Lawrence, Kansas, Exploring the City Sewer System, 1945

I was seven years old. My brother and his friend decided to pry up a manhole cover in the street and explore the sewers. All three of us descended the ladder fixed to the inside wall of the manhole. As we explored the sewer, we saw things we should not have seen, accompanied by strong odors. We walked about a block or so in the sewer pipe and looked up. There was a rectangle of light that turned out to be the opening for a street drain.

In 1943, only elderly people were out because the young men were off fighting the wars in Europe and Japan. There was a bus stop adjacent to the street drain, and many people were waiting for the bus. Looking up from inside the sewer, my brother and his friend masterminded a plan. They thought it would be fun if I, the youngest of the three, would yell, "Help I fell into the sewer, and I'm lost!"

That sounded like fun, so I yelled as loudly as I could. I faked crying out loud. Faces appeared upside down in the opening above us. After we started the commotion, we ran back to where we'd pried off the manhole cover and climbed out, replacing the cover.

Then we went back to the bus stop where I yelled my plea for help from the sewer below. We saw senior citizens talking to a policeman who had joined them. We got close enough to hear them tell the policeman about the kid who was lost in the sewer. We sensed that we had caused big trouble and quickly went home.

Shortly after the above venture, my mother married a man by the name of Bill Schindler. He had two daughters. One was sixteen years old, and the other was eighteen. We moved into the Schindler home.

This was a step up for us because Bill had a new Oldsmobile, and the home was two stories, with three bedrooms upstairs. It had just one central bathroom. The yard was very large. My brother and I took advantage of the yard. Since the location was just a block from the Kansas University stadium, each time there was a football game, we parked cars in our yard. We charged thirty-five cents to park in the yard. We collected enough money to go to the football game and have all the Cokes and hot dogs we could eat.

Another prank in Lawrence. As I saw cars coming to a stop at a stop sign, I ran up to the car and yelled, "Hey, mister, your rear wheel is rolling forward!" I pointed over and over at the rear wheel.

They always jumped out of the car and went to look at their rear wheel. Then they looked at me, got back in the car, and drove away.

My brother and I explored the trash cans at Kansas University and found many treasures. One day we found a slightly damaged full-size white plaster of paris bust of Benjamin Franklin. We took it home and thought about painting it with glow-in-the-dark paint, which was available by mail order ads in comic books. My brother had the brilliant idea of painting Benjamin Franklin's head with the luminous paint except around the eyes, nose, and ears. It would look like a glowing skull when the lights were out. Lights out, a glowing skull, lights on it was obviously Benjamin Franklin. We placed the bust in the middle of our stepsister's bed and closed the door. Both stepsisters were on dates that night. Mother, our stepfather, my brother, and I were in bed asleep when we heard a death-defying scream from the central hallway.

Everyone gathered in the upstairs hallway. Our stepsister had opened the door to the bedroom and saw the glowing skull. When she turned on the light, she saw Benjamin Franklin's bust on the bed. My stepfather turned off the light and saw the glowing skull. He was not happy! Following came a very angry inquisition. When he asked, "Who is responsible for this?" my brother and I pointed at each other. We thought our project was creative and funny, but no one else agreed.

Not long after that disastrous prank, Mother got a divorce and a better job working as a personal secretary for an air force colonel in Wichita, Kansas. We moved there without any sorrow on our departure.

I Pranked My Mother, Wichita, Kansas, 1949

Mother was invited to a dinner party and brought my brother and myself along. I overheard Mother tell her friend, "My son Doug has a huge bladder. He sure can pee for a long time." I thought about it and took it as an opportunity for some fun.

At home a couple of days later, I filled a large tea pitcher with water and went into the bathroom. I left the door cracked open about an inch, knowing my mother was in the next room. I emptied my bladder and then continued the trickling sound by slowly pouring the pitcher of water into the toilet. The trickling sound went on for a long, long time. Mother came, threw the door open, and caught me in the act with the nearly empty pitcher in hand. Strangely, she did not laugh.

Oxnard, California, 2008

My last prank on my mother was late in her life. By then, her sense of humor was mostly gone. So I thought I would cheer her up. I had just purchased a new Dodge Durango truck and arranged to take her to lunch.

After lunch, I helped her out of the truck at her home. I had the remote control for the truck door lock in my pocket. When I pushed the door-lock button on the remote, the truck's horn would beep.

I said, "This truck has such a sensitive security system that if I just touch the truck anywhere, it will beep." I demonstrated this by touching the fender at the same time I pushed the door-lock button in my pocket.

The horn beeped. I did this several more times with variation in rhythm and at different places on the truck. Each time the horn beeped.

I asked my mother to touch the fender. When she did, I did not push the door-lock button on the remote, so the horn didn't beep. I said, "Try it again." She touched it again. Nothing! I touched the fender and beeped the horn. I said, "I don't know what's wrong with your touch." I touched it again, and it beeped. We shrugged it off, and I walked with her up to her front door. I said, "I bet I can even just gesture by throwing a touch at the truck and it will still beep." I did this several times, and each time it beeped. She threw a pointed finger at the truck, but there was never a sound from the truck. Finally, I showed her how I was pushing the remote locking button to honk the horn. She nearly fell down laughing. This is the picture I took that day.

I have experienced the visions and now have a better understanding of how they function. Now I use the source as my constant contact in my daily life and defer to it when I need guidance.

Visions are not restricted by distance or time.

By the power of suggestion, a vision of an object, a city, or a planet can be visited anytime or anyplace.

Through the same source, I have visited several past lives and seen details with control over some aspects of the vision.

Printed in the United States
By Bookmasters